30 STRATEGIES
OF VIRAL MARKETING

GUIDE TO MARKETING

EARN HOW TO PROMOTE YOUR PRODUCTS ON SOCIAL WEB VIRALLY, REACH MILLIONS OF VISITORS IN A SHORT TIME.

BOETHIUS ANTHONY

30 STRATEGIES OF VIRAL MARKETING

Guide to Marketing

author

Boethius Anthony

lulu.com

© Copyright 2016 Boethius Anthony

Responsible for the publication Boethius Anthony

Book published at the expense of the author

[All right reserved]

Reproduction in any process of duplication of publications protected by copyright is prohibited and punishable by law (art. 171 of the Act of 22 April 1941 no. 633). This opera is protected under copyright law and international conventions for the protection of copyright (Berne Convention, Geneva Convention).

No part of this publication may therefore be reproduced, stored or transmitted by any means and in any form without the written permission of the publisher, except for the use of brief quotations in a book review or scholarly journal.

In any case of playback abuse will proceed of office in accordance with law.

_____

The author is a member of the site

lulu.com

ISBN 978-1-326-75672-7

www.jobboj.com

Summary

Preface VIII

1	Viral videos: the advantages 1
2	Viral videos and their business....................................... 3
3	The basics of viral videos.. 6
4	A winner formula for viral marketing............................ 8
5	The framework and discipline of viral marketing 11
6	Viral marketing for small businesses........................... 13
7	Using Facebook for viral marketing 16
8	Twitter as a prospective viral marketing strategy...... 18
9	Using greeting cards for viral marketing..................... 21
10	Top mistakes in viral marketing 23
11	Using Reddit for viral marketing 26
12	How to make a professional video for viral marketing 28
13	Features of a good viral video 31
14	Top websites for viral marketing 33
15	Marketing off viral E-books 36
16	Viral marketing: how is it different from direct marketing......... 38
17	SEO tools in viral marketing 41

18	Creating a viral Facebook Application	44
19	How to increase your website ranking	47
20	How to increase viral marketing for online store	49
21	Viral marketing for articles	52
22	Viral marketing via Instagram	54
23	Hiring an agency for viral marketing	57
24	Utilising free viral marketing Application	60
25	Boost viral marketing of Blogs	62
26	Viral marketing with Youtube	65
27	Viral marketing of Music	67
28	Viral marketing for amateurs	70
29	Event promotion and destination marketing	72
30	Best Photos for viral marketing	75

Preface

A book written by a marketer and made for marketers.

For those starting their business online, or a new career: a complete text of useful tips concerning the world of viral marketing, a little guide to read and maintain.

Therefore, it is suitable for both novice and future marketers, as for those already working from home and want to improve their skills, searching for a "perfect strategy" for their needs, make themselves known quickly and promote their products.

A book...

    written for your business...

        absolutely, to read!

ANTHONY BOETHIUS

The Art Of Viral Marketing

1   Viral videos: the advantages

Making viral videos for the purpose of telemarketing and more importantly internet marketing is nowadays the most valuable pathway to go down on. It is the safest and yet the most attracting of all the options you have for showing off and advertising your brand or company. Of the innumerable advantages that viral videos have over other modalities, some of the most important are as follows.

Viral videos are inexpensive

There is a minimal cost of developing and creating a video for this purpose and putting it out live to get it viral. You can literally start with absolutely nil investment in the start by making use of the various social platforms available at your disposal. **There is no upload cost at all.**

As your goals get upgraded towards higher benefits and thresholds, you can choose to get your videos uploaded and run on other more popular media for a greater exposure.

That will guarantee a greater audience and an eager population appealed towards your brand or product.

Viral videos are the key to future prospects

There was a time when images were the focus of major companies and brand sellers. In the modern century, the starting imagery and even covers of products have largely been replaced by videos to provide a life like summary of the importance of the product. A trailer of no matter how **short a duration** is always given preference over imagery of any sort.

Viral videos can be humorous

You can add various levels of humor in your viral videos which will produced emotional attraction among the audience. So instead of an audience bored by the bullet points of your great idea, there will be some eye catching theme which will improve the attention span and quality of your audience. This also ensures the viral part of your campaign. Today most people use the many social sites and it is widely appreciated that **humor content is the most shared among groups**. So this ensures that your video is not limited a single or local group of audience but spread to afar.

Viral videos are entertaining

The videos are focused on the basic idea behind it but the convey system it is based on gets the most gazes. People are looking out for more and more entertaining stuff and they will literally stop for only things like that. It is very much appreciated from the example of *ALS Bucket Challenge video*. It has grossed over a hundred million dollars and that is only for its entertainment part and the fun aspect that got people to rise for once off their sitting positions and do something exciting.

These are some of the many advantages of the viral videos to engage a viral audience for your company, brand or product of any sorts. This is to guarantee you a selling edge over other modalities.

2 Viral videos and their business

Viral videos or video marketing is an out of ordinary way of advertising a name or brand over multiple and rather diverse platforms. In other words it is an unconventional method. But as is the fact this is the most

attractive mode of displaying to the world what you love. Unlike the basic summaries of names which show an extensive analysis on the subject a video is an interactive session live display of the product with elements of excitement fun and occasionally humor. Most videos are shared of the many popular social interfaces used nowadays which ensures that it is seen by all no matter on which corner of the world they are.

There are various ways of spreading the video online

Perhaps the most important one used is **YouTube**. It is credible and has the greatest number of people watching it at a time in the world. The server is secure and has minimal kinks and flaws. There has been shown that most people nowadays used chart based rating systems for their video searching rather than a usual typing for keyword search. This will produce the most popular searches on the top so that your video after receiving the necessary audience will remain to be highest watching video of all times and thus continue spreading.

Viral videos have several edges over customary methods

These videos will produce a much clearer and sharper impact for your advertised product. Other than the fact that they provide definite answers to costumers, these videos are also used widely for their appealing and attracting powers. Find the right information through a ritual of fun and entertainment is an ideal for people. These videos are also good at being limitless in their prowess of time and space. They can be watched multiple times, at any time and at any place. These provides convenience and thus an easy going for the customers,

Viral videos are to be monitored for their trending

This means that it is to be ensured that you check each and every day for the charts and ratings for your videos to know how much of an appeal they are making out in the open. This not only makes you gain experience points for your future projects, but also helps you to make decisions about your current postings. You can choose to edit your posted video to make it more attractive or even remove one if it is in your best interest.

It is true that viral videos have not yet taken the spot for television commercials and other modalities but one thing is clear. It is here to stay and grow beyond its current boundaries. This is why most people and entrepreneurs are turning over to this in increasing numbers for their day to day advertisements. The prospect for viral videos is huge and is definitely going to increase in the coming years.

3 The basics of viral videos

Viral videos are videos on the internet that are so well spread among a large population that it gets highlighted across multiple platforms. Most of the videos are shot by amateurs at times when something funny is going on and on uploading them, they become increasingly viral. YouTube is currently the biggest platform where these videos get there necessary audience to be ranked as a viral video. They even get to a point that these start getting to be talked about at various talk shows around the globe and gain even more popularity.

If you want to get some focus on a product or a brand you are selling, a viral video can be a great help towards its publicity and awareness. But as it is, there are points to be looked at before making sure that a video goes viral over the social hub of today's internet.

The attention span of the audience is generally very small. People like to view videos which are short and quick to reach a necessary climax. A video that is usually longer than 30 seconds is too long. Now it is true to think about how is it possible to accumulate all the data in such short interval. But the important thing is to increase the popularity and audience of your video first.

You have to make sure that your video is not a commercial. Viewers are not interested in that and will only stick to your video if it is more than just a simple straight forward advertisement. So it is important to put fun ideas into it that indirectly lead that the viewers to think about your product.

Make sure your video is pretty to look at. The choice of the people who are taking part in the video making is utmost. The background, the scenery and the objectivity should be pleasing to the eyes.

It is also essential that the video is shocking in a way. That means your video must have an appalling climax edge to it. That heightens the emotions of the audience and compels them to not only watch it again but also share it with the people around them on social platforms.

Make a video that can be used again. Your video should be able to be accommodated in other prospects as per your audience. This will make your video travel on various different leagues and promote its spread and popularity.

Accomplishing all this will make sure that the odds are in your favor. But it doesn't still confirm for you a hundred percent success on it. You have to rely on all the rest of marketing skills you have and get your video out to the blogs, social websites and email audiences. If it is a very good one, it might create a storm of itself but usually it is more difficult to achieve. It requires a lot of patience and hard work to achieve it on a large enough scale so that your video to be called viral.

4   A winner formula for viral marketing

Viral marketing the best and easiest way to ensure a snowball effect for the increased awareness of your brand or product. There are many sites available that are purely present to help you achieve this goal of yours. Websites like YouTube, Facebook and Flickr are built to be viral. Viral marketing makes sure that

you get an exponential increase in the viral internet traffic of your product. This leads to an increase in the usage of your product which in turns lead to an increase search list rating and thus continuing the cycle of popularity In a positive direction.

Consider making a viral marketing not a viral product. This is to make sure that with each user viewing your product, a new user is linked to the chain of ongoing sharing. On the other hand if you just focus on your product being viral, the spreading on of your information halts to a standstill. The user will use it but the message will stop reaching out of the zone.

Make a free offer. A free offer is almost always irresistible to the viewer. Even for those audience who are not interested in buying the product, will be very much attracted to the offer. The word free is almost always a success in itself.

Target the viral users. This pertains to those audiences that are more in the habit of spreading out the message across. These spread not only the message fast but also to a wider span of audience.

Be ahead of others. It is probable that the idea you have is exactly like the one so many people around the globe have. So it is important to stand out amongst your competition and provide a reason for the audience to choose your product instead of the countless others. You have to be thus more creative and knowledgeable and should have the right marketing resources at your disposal.

The transfer methods you deploy should be easy. You have to use the existing social platforms as they are the working foundation of your marketing journey. You have to choose the fastest method which has the greatest probability of working great and achieving success.

Use other's resources. It is easier and better to deploy your advertisements on other websites so that the traffic is organized in a balance between your and the rest of the websites. This lessens the burden and increases the growth.

Be prepared for a large traffic. The resources you have employed should have the ability to be optimized for a larger response if and when needed. There should be automated responders instead of manual answering because the feasibility quickly lessens as a new user is affiliated to your group.

With this in mind, there is little doubt left for any damages and a continuous stream of potential response is initiated quickly. You will be able to achieve the heights of viral marketing for your brand or product in sooner than ever.

5   The framework and discipline of viral marketing

Viral marketing is a term that is used almost invariably loosely today in regards to many other modalities. It is in fact a living channel on its own when it takes the form of a transporter of great data flow across the globe through internet. Also there is a clear cut distinction between viral and viral marketing. Anything can go viral but if an element of focus towards a certain important object or concept is added, it is marketing that has gone viral. Following is a summary about what it actually is about.

There are a number of misconceptions about viral marketing

Viral marketing is not just about adding a share button to your content. Sharing does not make your stuff viral. Although it is big part of its promotion, it doesn't ensure the successful outcome. Similarly, using the basic websites like Facebook and YouTube are not confirmations on your viral marketing. They are a great foundation but not the only prerequisite.

Viral as a word today is almost invariably used with video. Although it is part of the ever increasing trend nowadays, it is not the case. Anything can go viral be it a photo or an article. Videos are just thus part of a bigger picture of how the viral marketing actually plays its role in our daily lives.

Also viral not necessarily means a set number of hits for example 100,000. It is purely based on a predetermined number according to particular sets of data and requirement.

Viral literally is the biological entity you all know of

It is distinct because it has the ability to self-replicate in increased numbers over time. Viral marketing is not a newfound entity but has been in demand for a long time. What has changed is the methodology of it via increased available modes and platforms over which viral marketing takes place. This is new to the basic past scheme of email forwarding method.

Viral marketing is based on three channels

The most important part of it is the entertainment factor. To get the attention span of your audience by your viral marketed product, you have to make it eye *catching* and *fun*. Your creativity plays the part in it to make it stand among the others and prove beneficial.

Viral marketing goes beyond the critical threshold level even faster when there are giveaways involved. You can give your time in case it is about providing a service. You can on the other hand offer free or discounted stuff in case there are goods involved.

A new and unique idea is quick to get everybody's attention. People love to share the concept which is new in the market and thus the popularity of your viral marketed product is sure to rise many folds.

All that is left is a perfect execution of all your plans

You need to plan ahead about all the available resources at your disposal and the methodologies that you can employ to create the perfect score for your viral marketing. You have to know about the potential of the social platforms that you are using and go about with it. Together you will have the perfect recipe for the perfect viral marketing.

6   Viral marketing for small businesses

Viral marketing is the choice of most companies nowadays because of its high rate of success for the company's products. But it is not always the beneficiary.

Some companies just let it go out of their hands and the motions spiral out of control. It is also believed that viral marketing is pretty expensive campaign to run so it is limited to only the biggest and richest companies of all. This notion is wrong and small business can have a huge burst of growth using the advantages of viral marketing.

It is all about the perfect timing

Viral marketing is to use the right resources at the right time for the right purpose. This means to use what little you have in the most efficient way so none is wasted and maximum yield is acquired.

It is **easy to use** as you are using your customers to do the viral marketing for you. It all then comes down to whether they are happy with your product or not. And if you can manage to provide them a fairly good deal, you are sure to increase your growth.

There should be **no need to explain** your product to others. When the customers can just send their friends or family a link to your marketing channel, it makes things easier. On the other hand if one has to provide details himself to others, it will be negated most of the times. This is the background behind a good viral video as the user just has to share a good video with someone instead of telling him or her about the contents of the video itself.

The channel should have a **lowest requirement** for members. This means to create a platform where there is individuality instead of a community needing. If a user is asked to bring in at least for example 10 of his friends with him, there is most probably a chance of rejecting the medium altogether.

The viral marketing platform that you have provided to your users should be filled with a good **background of entertainment** and fun. This ensures that the audience doesn't see it as a means of a simple advertisement and rather a cool part where they are enjoying themselves. This also increases the attention span of the users initiating the thought provoking center in them about your product.

Buzz marketing can also be implicated in your approach to viral marketing

You do not need to have a wonderfully crafted product for this. If you can manage to create enough hype or buzz about it, you can amass enough interested audience for you. A catchy advertisement that is focused on your product is just the right thing for you to lead on.

Viral marketing can also be easily employed on an offline manner. You can promote your small business by handed out some free items in return for your customers to bring out more of their friends and family. An offer put out for the guests will keep the cycle turning.

7 Using Facebook for viral marketing

Viral marketing has reached a great expanse in the latest years. From campaigns to simple marketing of products and descriptions, viral marketing is providing the best framework. There are a lot of social websites for promotion of your brand or product. Among others, the usefulness of Facebook has far outreached others. It was created as a social and bonding site about 10 years ago and has brought in users from almost all the corners of the world in one place. There are literally no geographical boundaries to hinder the flow of information. A message spreads quickly among friends and family and then the successor kith and kin. The expansion is exponential. Following are usage descriptions of the most vital of the websites features.

The profile page is the basis of your character on Facebook. You have to appreciate the fact the viral marketing over the internet is essentially a word of mouth. So all that goes up on your profile page is the basis for your audience to define you. Make it short and simple. Put all your important descriptions in it and make it cool.

A friend list is the basis of your market channeling. You can start by importing your contact list from any of your email addresses and then starting on them. Afterwards you have the ability to contact the friends of your friends or simply rely on the suggestions provided by Facebook itself.

The personal message option is to be used as much as can be. You can use to congratulate your viewers on their personal ceremonies and give a touch of personal connection with them. This builds trust which is one of the important pillars of viral marketing.

You can post photos and videos

They provide the core of your viral marketing campaign. These provide the life and a sense of excitement to your product. They capture people's attention and make the most impact on their emotional centers. This means better response leading to increased sharing ahead. In advance photos can be tagged with your companies name which increases awareness. Additionally the photos of your customers can be posted on your wall and they can be tagged in them which confers an increased connection between you and your client.

The comments section provides an essential feedback. As you post a product, people either have questions about it beforehand or those who have used it will have general views about it to share to others. It is your job to keep yourself in the loop so that you can remove any doubts and misunderstandings. You can keep all of your audience informed and direct them towards the right direction.

There is an excellent option to make additional pages. You can keep them all updated and centered on a single focus of attention. And yet you can display multiple aspects of your campaign in those pages to organize it all in a better way.

8 Twitter as a prospective viral marketing strategy

Twitter is the next best thing today. It is social platform to meet new people and update your social life or you can utilize it to be your viral marketing foundation. Titter is even so popular

nowadays that most celebrities also use it. This is due to the security details that it provides to its customers. Twitter makes sure that the user of the account is real and thus maintains the authenticity of its audience. This ensures a secure and valid channeling for everything that goes around there.

Opening several accounts on twitter is not the best trick. The key is to have a central account with several accounts directed towards it. This maintains the security and legal details and keeps you away from the ramifications of being expelled.

The most important thing that you have to begin with is your bio. Twitter even generates a bio for you if you have not provided one. But it is to provide one yourself just the way you want it to be. You can add your picture and define your qualities and your designated services.

The whole marketing circulates around your tweets. You have to keep posting from time to time so that your audience is kept in the loop. This will keep them involved and increase their interest in your idea. Also with your increasing number of tweets, they will have new stuff to retweet and share it to others and thus expand your marketing circle.

It is also important to create a twitter link for your work. This means to add an extension for your twitter account on anything that you post elsewhere. It could be blogs or videos posted online through other channels. People like a link where they can always be updated on what new you have to bring out to them.

One thing that you can employ to your aid is tagging. That means to create the markers relates to your product or idea so that everything remains related to the main idea. Much like the game of childhood, tag and you are it, this ensures a steady but continuous channeling where more and more people are aware about your viral marketing campaign.

Twitter is more about the personal you and less as you the head of the company. So make sure you provide the personal vibe and let fun and entertainment also flow in on your work. This keeps people interested and amazed at all the new and better stuff that you intend to provide them.

9 Using greeting cards for viral marketing

Viral marketing is so powerful a tool that it surpasses all the past advancements in marketing and render them obsolete. Search engines and link exchanges look almost insignificant in front of it. Viral marketing is about creating something amazing and sharing it among a few. Then it is their job to spread it to others and create a never ending expansion of your liking focused on you as the center. This is the viral characteristic which likes a real life virus. It infects a few cells and the progeny infects furthermore cells.

The only difference is that in this case the people who like something share it with others and they spread it further. And also that here we want our marketing to get infected quickly. The beauty of it lies in the little investment resulting into large profits.

One important way to start and accomplish this mission of viral marketing is to **use greeting cards.** The basic concept of it is of a website that lets the user to create a greeting card and send it to anybody he or she desires. It can be customized in any way as is desired. The writing can be changed, an audio file attached and animation added. The receiver of the email is granted a link which when opened, displays the greeting card to the viewer. Plus now with the website's link at the disposal of the receiver, he or she can use it to send greeting cards to others.

So all that is left for you is to **create good enough greeting cards** to begin with. If you can do that and get the attention of the first batch of the customers, the process ahead is self-automated and you can sit back and relax. But as easy as it looks like, it is not that simple. You really need great ideas to start so that people have something that stands out from the rest of the lot. Sharing your website with people for the first is also hard, let alone getting them to use it. You can use the many social websites at your disposal to work this initial hurdle.

The good way to market your website is to **market the greeting cards** in it. Make sure that all your cards are displayed in all the search engines. But first begin with choosing one or two themes about your website. When you have done that, search for the necessary resource material like photos and animations to put on your cards. Make sure that you respect the copyrights of everything.

You then have the option to either create a service yourself on your site or choose an existing **greeting card service.** The second option is the easier of the two and so an ideal for a beginner. As you grow you can change to the self-maintaining of your website. You can then just sit and concentrate on the editing of the resource material and tailor it to your needs. The forms for the cards will be submitted to your sites and they will channeled in making the cards. You can also respond on your site for any queries and solve any issues.

Once started it is sure to expand in no time and increase the traffic on your site.

10 Top mistakes in viral marketing

Viral marketing is a big selling strategy if it is employed perfectly. But on the other the hand if overlooked and the basics ignored then all the resources you may have spent on your marketing may go to complete waste. Among the many others these are the most common of the mistakes made in viral marketing.

Most people fail to produce it adequately interesting

If you haven't made a piece as interesting and full of entertainment as it was supposed to be, you will not

get the necessary attention of your audience. This is true even if you decide to invest more of your resources on the project. On the other hand an interesting item will sell even without the spending that much capital.

Viral marketing faces a major hurdle also when you can't provide incentives for sharing ahead. This means to provide the customers with offers like money, services or discounts for their sharing of the message ahead. People don't find a need to do viral marketing for you when there is no profit for them in it.

Similarly if you fail to provide them the right incentive to respond to your product, the cycle would never start. This means to display an offer at the end of your description where the people are motivated to gather around the focus of attention that you have provided them. You have to make sure that the offer is related to your field of interest, or else there will be a lot of contacts that you have to filter out.

Some people assume too much. You must not stop encouraging people about responding to your campaign and spreading it ahead. Statistics about the traffic on your site should be carefully evaluated. Audience should be pursued to continue to share the status ahead to new people.

You must not focus more on the marketing piece

Rather the process of viral marketing should be brought into the spotlight. It is possible that a very good piece is not recognized entirely and a simple object be appreciated worldwide. It all depends on the level of viral marketing channeling.

You must not make the mistake of leaving the project before you have learnt something new from the moments you experienced. You must always track the results so that you know your weakness and what you have to do next. Those who fail to do that keep on making the same mistakes over and over again and their viral marketing is a disaster at their own hands.

Another common mistake is to make the preparations less than what should have been done. This is because most people have little self-confidence and no can-do attitude towards themselves. So just make sure that you send invitations as if it were a blockbuster film. This puts you in a no risk zone and make sure that the increase in traffic is twofold to what is expected.
Keeping these in mind will get you to the top of the viral marketing in no time.

11 Using Reddit for viral marketing

Viral marketing is easy to follow at the various social websites at your disposal like Facebook and twitter. But if you want to gear your produce up a notch, Reddit provides the platform for that improvement. Reddit is a website that is all about the content delivery and presentation. It is one of the most popular and widely seen website in the world.

It is all about posting new and unique content that the world will acclaim or refuse.

Decide carefully what to post. Your content should be distinctively interesting and captivating. There should be the elements of being funny, smart and at the same time increasingly intellectual. You will have to decide on which tone to use at an individual basis depending on the topic of the content that you are posting.

The audience of this site is a bit different. They are much more involved in the quality of the content than just focusing on the entertainment part of the post. Thus a good post will quickly get the attention of the readers and the necessary fame resulting into accumulation of the needed karma points. On the other hand if they don't find it worthwhile, the users will be fast in making sure that your content is pulled off the website using the bad remarks and comments that they put up.

You can use the voting system to increase the odds in your favor. As you post interesting posts on the site, you can open polls to get the vote of the current users. This will prove to be very beneficial when you get the positive reviews with the voting. This leads to the necessary traffic to your content.

Use Reddit advertisements

When you see yourself at a place where you can take a great leap forward towards success, you can choose to opt for ads on the site. There is a great scope of putting your ads up on Reddit and getting the greatest traffic for your campaign. But this is one of the last steps towards your way to fame and glory.

There is great trend of gift sharing on Reddit. Be sure to participate in this generous act of love among the users of Reddit. This will make your work a lot easy. You will be counted as one of their own and the content that you post will gain the necessary exposure much faster.

Be aware of the many subreddits. These are the applications of the various subcommittees towards grouping the content. Find the necessary ones which are generous and not too targeted or political. A judicious use of the subreddits is indicated.

There are many other features you can put to great use. Use the Reddit tips which provide useful information towards making your progress easier. Imgur is an associated site which hosts images on Reddit. Other important features that you can explore further are Radio Reddit, University Reddit and Job Reddit.

12. How to make a professional video for viral marketing

Viral marketing is available on a variety of different platforms. But the main essence that might be left out when campaigning for the best, is a video.
A video sparks the life in your viral marketing cycle.

It brings out the more creative part of you outside in the open and makes you stand out among your competitors. There are many ways to create a good video that will make a good focus of attention but as with anything else that is new, you will always some basic steps and guidelines to help you get started. Video making has always been a tiring and troublesome task for the beginners but as soon as you make your first video, you can keep going forever. Here is how to get started.

There are a few basic things that you will require

Although you will find that there are in fact many instruments and upgrades that you can use but to get started in a well-organized manner, there are only a few that really are needed. You will require a good video camera that can be connected to a computer, a personal computer, a tripod stand, a connecting cable and a well-lit place.

1. **Now connect the camera to the computer, preferably via a Firewire cable.** Launch windows movie maker which is pre-installed on almost personal computers running windows xp and higher versions. Make sure you are in a well-lit room.
2. **Record the video via the capture button.** The video that you have made will automatically be saved on the timeline of the video maker.

3. **The most important part is the editing.** This is the level where it is determined whether your video is up to the mark or not. The windows movie maker provides ample options to edit your video according to your liking. You can drag your video on the available timeline and cut it to remove the parts you do not want present. You can also add sound files over the video wherever and howsoever you want. The video can also be edited to combine different effects, filters and enhancements. There is also the option to add self-made templates in between the video to highlight necessary points, make headers or simply a continuation of the different parts of the video.
4. **Save the video.** When asked, choose the best resolution available to have a video that will look good even on a larger screen.
5. **Upload the video according to your preference.** There are various social websites that you can avail to your benefit to gain the traffic for your newly created viral video.

At the start, there might be a slow rise in the liking of your video. But this just a phase you have to pass through. Afterwards, you can better decide the settings for your videos and even get the support of better and more professional instruments and software.

13. Features of a good viral video

Viral marketing has reached a new skyline following the advent of the release of viral videos over the internet. The traffic for your advertisement campaign is bound to reach much higher levels if great videos are included in it. The videos that become viral nowadays belong to a diverse group of genre ranging from funny to shocking and from accidental to professionally made videos. All the videos even though different in their own sense, fulfills the criteria of a good video and thus reach greater levels of attention and publicity.

The most important criteria for a good viral video is its length. The preferred length is usually between *2 to 3 minutes*. This if taken into greater consideration is also the time of the commercials that we see on television. This is because any longer than this and the people start losing all the interest in it and even if they do see it all, they cannot focus the subject of the video completely.

Another big factor is the picture quality of the video made. Most video makers find it handy and easy to record a video from their phones and quickly upload it from there. This only works well enough on a pretty small scale of viral video marketing. As you grow up a level, you need to work with a better camera so that a decent video is made.

Similarly the audio quality of the video matters too. Too faint or too loud is not desirable in a video. The audio should be clear and there should be minimal noise present. This makes the understanding easier for the audience and promotes the publicity.

The main part of the video is centered on the content. It should be polite and should contain the elements of joy, entertainment and emotions. Simultaneously it should be able to deliver the intended message clearly and easily. The audience expects it to be simple and easy to understand in a good video.

As described above the message should be crystal clear. The main theme of the video should be easy to grasp and share with others. Any video that is made by linking together bits of other videos and have little sense of meaning to it are not the right sort of videos.

An important part of the viral videos on the internet are somehow useful to people. These videos which teach people a short skill or activity always grow exponentially in the sharing audience. People love to gain more knowledge and these types of videos deliver just that in a more fun and initiative way.

There are many software available for good video making. Some of the good ones are Easy Video Suite, The Traffic Player and Tuber Toolbox. These applications provide ample editing tools to make a great video. Every site has its own special pros and cons. You can research on them to know exactly which one is best suited for the job.

14   Top websites for viral marketing

Viral marketing has reached a great horizon in the recent past. It has taken on different shapes including viral videos, viral photos, viral cards, viral article and a lot more. This has become enabled due to the many great websites that let the users post new campaigns swiftly and easily and at the same time provide the readers of the site an interface that provides them utmost

comfort ability and pleasure in viewing the viral content.
- **BuzzFeed** is at the top with over a hit score of 260,000,000. It was launched in 2006 and provides content including news, entertainment and viral content to be shared across the globe.
- **Vox** is a great platform that not only allows for the posting of viral content but also a social networking stage.
- **UpWorthy** is a website that provides viral video and graphical content to be shared.
- **Mic** aims to explain what is happening around us, why is it occurring and how it is proceeding through time.
- **Thought Catalog** is an independently run website that stores people's ideas and creativity and share them among various groups for better understanding.
- **Distractify** lets you explore the vastness of the many cultures around the world. You can read countless stories and strike for limitless educational entertainment.
- **Laughing Squid** is daily increment of distinctive culture, technology and art. It will always keep your fun part of the brain lighted up.
- **Fail Blog** is the best single stage with the biggest collection of fails from around the world. It is sure to keep you giggling and laughing hard.
- **CEOWORLD magazine** is as the name suggests. It is the hub of the elite of the business lot and serves what is

new in that world. Read every day for the latest updates, it is a must for your developing campaigns and deciding the future of it.
- **Cracked** is a huge bundle of facts that are covered with humor and laughter. It is sure to keep you going for hours.

These were some of the best ongoing **viral websites** that provide a lot of content for reading and viewing. For those who are starting in their long run of viral marketing, they will find these social networks much easier at first.
- **Facebook** is the leading social platform which provides you with ample opportunities for starting a good viral marketing campaign.
- **YouTube** is as is evident the best place to share good viral videos and share them across the globe.
- **Myspace** provides you with an entertainment filled experience through a great deal of viral content.
- **LinkedIn** is a professional website that is suited for those who want to share and gain experience in the skilled class.
- **Twitter** is focused on micro blogging. It is much secured website which has compelled to include the most notable of celebrities.
- **Flicker** is a social website that is related to photographic content from various fields including news, entertainment and other important categories.

- **Hi5** lets you connect with people from around the world for free. It not only links those who know each other but also with new unknown people so they may get to know each other.

15   Marketing off viral E-books

Viral marketing has taken many shapes and forms from videos to articles. There is a lot pf prospect in campaigning with *viral E-books*.

1. **The major advantage of going with viral e-books is the cost effectiveness.**
   There is almost no or minimal initial investment. The only major cost id of using the software that is needed to compile the e-book. There are many formats that you can use for your viral e-book. You can chooses from exe, doc or pdf formats. But it is much preferable to choose

pdf as it compatible with both windows and mac so there will be bigger audience your work. There are even ways to convert your files to pdf for free so this initial cost is also out of the equation.
2. **The second reason for using viral e-books is the potential for massive exposure.** It is difficult to initiate a larger audience in case of a printed book. It usually stays in the local community for a longer period of time. As opposed to this an e-book can be quickly circulated among many different diverse groups around the globe. Thus there are higher chances of finding an audience that is very much interested in reading your work and appreciating you for your effort.
3. **The third major advantage of using an e-book is the branding of your name.** When you get a number of people reading your book, you have that same number of people knowing your name and be associated with you. This means that now they are familiar a brand and if they love your initial work, they would love to get from you. This is the method that has led to so many names over the internet to become so massively popular.

There are many ways to start writing a good book and making sure it gets the attention and focus it deserves

Some important tips hereby mentioned will give you a good enough boost for your marketing of the viral e-books.

The book that you write should be at least once **proof read** before it is published online. This ensures that it is in a perfect shape and that you do not have to go over the failure of your work. Through this any mistakes are removed and your work is polished to look shiny and better.

Make sure that the **style** of your e-book is perfectly in line with the audience that you intent for it. This means to use any photographic or animations tools at your disposal to make the cover of your book look life like and close to an actual book. This urges the readers to prefer it to other books on the internet.

It is important to choose the right **length, size and format** of your e-book. Keeping your viral e-book short for up to about 18 to 20 pages is preferred as this is the ideal size for most people on the internet.

Finally make sure that you put the link for your e-book on multiple sites and pages of social sites so that the element of **viral marketing** is brought into good use.

16 Viral marketing: how is it different from direct marketing

Marketing is an essential specialization in today's world for almost all the businesses around. It means to convey and convince the audience to buy a product or follow an enterprise through any means viable and necessary. There are many ways to classify and divide the marketing schemes but the major categories are direct and viral marketing.

Direct marketing is the usual way for most companies that have been running around for a long time. It involves direct communication with the potential customers and providing them the information about the product or brand name that is supposed to be sold. This method involves the use of direct modalities like *face to face conversation, flyers, brochures, mails and telephone calls*. This kind of communication does not rely on the passing on of the advertising information through intermediary channels. Direct marketing is attractive to companies in that it is easier to calculate the sales statistics. For examples if a sales person has made approximately 500 telephone calls and about 50 people have bought the product then the sales are about 10 percent.

Viral marketing on the other hand relies basically on the passing on of information through multiple secondary pathways to a greater and vast audience. It includes the use of the many social platforms available out there to spread the message far and across. Another important difference there is between viral and direct marketing is that the subject to send via viral marketing can be any ranging from blogs, articles, videos and images to products and services.

There are principally three different methodologies employed in viral marketing. The **word of mouth** technique is the most basic of them all. It is based on using a product or service and then passing on the general information regarding it to people including family and friends. It is mostly an opinion about the product or information based on the personal experience that the consumer had. The second methodology is the use of **social websites.** This is by far the most widely used method in viral marketing. The audience can be global in this endeavour. It is easier to use these websites and share the message across very easily and with just a few clicks. The third way of doing viral marketing is the **Invite your friends** technique. It is also a very popular approach in communicating to people other than the direct consumers of the product or service. After a customer has utilized an expertise, he or she is provided with an opportunity to invite friends and family to try and experience the same.

The **advantages of viral marketing** are many. There is a negligible or absolutely no investment at all. The growth is exponential in characteristic. This corresponds to the viral nature of this type of marketing. Just like a biological virus, the advertising information spreads through an audience, increasing the number of channels with each new information receiver. There can be inserted a tone of humour, fun and entertainment to the advertisement which gives a boost to the marketing sales.

17 SEO tools in viral marketing

Viral marketing takes on many shapes and foundations in its working over the internet. There are many modalities for sharing your content across a wide variety of audience globally. An important part of this marketing is to put up with the Search Engine Optimization standards so that your corresponding website is displayed and registered well in search engines. This is important in getting the link of your website in the top entries of keyword searches. There are many tools available for this. Some can be bought over the internet while others less professional are available free. Some of the important ones are discussed further here.

A must is the **Keyword Density Checker.** It is important to have your site being matched most frequently to the keywords searched online and this is where this tool comes

in. It calculates for you the required number of keywords that you need to put up in your content which ultimately favors a greater search pick out.

Another tool is the **Back link Finder.** It lets you find out exactly how much traffic of incoming links is there against a particular designated domain. This makes it easier for you to focus your strengths towards a favorable outcome.

Alexa Rank Checker is essential for confirming and following up on your sites performance. It is a website ranking tool that displays your current status in the competition out there.

A great tool is the **Mega Tag Analyzer.** It looks for the mega tags of the website and extracts them and helps you in determining the best keywords to choose for your website.

Domain IP Address Checker is a great tool. It locates and pinpoints the exact location of any incoming emails that are unwanted or loaded with a virus. You can track down the owner of any IP address, domain or website.

Compete Ranking Checker is able to determine the traffic of unique and characteristic visitors and viewers on your website. This directly corresponds to the rating that you will achieve among your audience over the Internet.

A similar tool is the **Google Page Rank Checker.** This took determines your position that had been allotted to your website by Google.

Word Count Tool held you to calculate the number of words that you have put in your content and able you to determine your progress.

With these tools you are sure to receive a great rank on based on the Search Engine Optimization protocols. Your website will be positioned high in the search results which means more clicks per one keyword search. This simplifies to a basic degree of viral marketing where your content is not only shared by direct passing on of the total information, but also via the related keywords.

18 Creating a viral Facebook Application

Viral marketing has taken on many shapes and forms in today's social buzz. One such aspect is the creation of applications on Facebook that has created a great hype over the past few years. Applications such as Movies, have already claimed an acclaimed fame in a short period with an enthusiastic global audience. Applications on Facebook are a great opportunity for you to start putting out your best in the easiest possible way to create a larger traffic to your website.

The most basic of the things you have to consider before you start making a Facebook application, is deciding the **type of application.** You can choose either a desktop or an over the web application. The difference lies in the fact that users will have to download the app in former while they will use the app online in latter.

The next part is to make an **interesting title** for your application. You have to create something that will stick in the minds and memory of people and they would love to share it with others with confidence. It should be fun and and easy

and comfortable to talk about.

There is a part about putting up the **description of your application.** Make a description that is easier to understand. It should highlight the main features of your application and at the same time describing to the users the functionality of your app. It should be mesmerizing enough to be able to convince the user to add that application of yours.

An **icon** for your application is also another concern. You can choose an image that is memorable and long lasting for the app's users. An icon is the like of a gate through which the users must pass through to explore what's inside.

After fulfilling the basic requirement of your Facebook application, you can start worrying about the actual stuff that goes in it. One of the popular features that is bound to receive positive reviews is **news feed.** This is like any other news feed that brings out new updates for users about the application on a daily basis. This not only keeps the users inside the loop but also brings out an environment where they get to experience something new everyday. You have to be careful about putting up the news feed. It should be clever, fun, exciting and entertaining for the users and not just every stuff you think you need to post. There should something unique and creative every time a user gets to read the news feed.

The application should have a really easy way of sending **requests and invites.** This is the basic step in getting your application to be shared across multiple channels to increase popularity. Usually there is a limit of sending 20 invites per day.

A key feature of a good application is good **notification service.** Notifications provide the users with healthy information about their current progression and convince them to choose your app over others.

You have to make sure that there is **no** spam being produced by your application so that it does not get blocked out of people's inbox. This means that no excessive amount of notifications be sent to non-application users or you would face blockages

An application is supposed to be acknowledged by minimum of starting 5 users before it is published by Facebook. If an application is thus drawn on these few basic concepts, there will be a sure response towards you and the traffic to your site would increase tremendously.

19 How to increase your website ranking

Viral marketing is an art of publishing your content and getting for it an almost global consideration through internet. An important criteria that governs the showcasing of your content over the Internet is the ranking generated for your website. There are many platforms which formulate a position for your site that transforms into the popularity that you receive.  Whatever the channel, the ranking of your content depends upon how well is the Search Engine Optimization of your website. There are many ways to achieve a higher profile in this category.

Articles directories are open to your postings. You can publish a blog on your website and then attach it to an article directory without editing it in any way. There is no penalisation for this and individual rules and regulations for particular directories can be looked for also.

Social media usage is a must for good viral marketing. You can post all your links to social websites like Facebook, LinkedIn and others. This makes the process of sharing your work with others much easier. There is however a caution specifically for Twitter. It is characterized by faster tweets that makes the reading span of a post really small. In this case, the trick is to break down the post to smaller multiple tweets corresponding to the content of your website.

Video making is a great to use technique in viral marketing. You can convert your articles into videos by making PowerPoint presentations and employing tools like Camtasia Studios to record screen. The videos can then be posted on YouTube which will generate an increased traffic to your website. Here again you have to make sure that the title you use for your video has the same keywords as those used in your website content. This will help to bring the rating of your website high up.

Audio and images are preferred by most people nowadays. They can put the mp3 files in their computers, phones and audio players and listen to them without having to leave something else important. This thus helps to promote your work in a much increasing frequency. Same goes for images in regards to their flexible use and versatility. You must ensure that you put an image next to and related to a particular keyword so that the searches of your audience are always matched to your work.

Slideshows are also a great feature to upload with your writings. There are many great tools available like

Slideshare to upload and share your slideshows over the internet. This is an intuitive way to bring out something new and unique in the marketing business.

Documents are also important to be published in correct formats via PDFs mostly. Sites like *Scribd* are especially suited for posting these documents.

This looks like a lot of work if you are new to the concept of viral marketing. However there are great tools and services available to help you out in this endeavour. *Pixelpipe* is one the great services that allow you to easily post and publish your content in the form of documents, audio, videos and much more.

20 How to increase viral marketing for online store

Online stores are a great potential in today's market and an increasing number of people are already opening new everyday. This form of selling products has greatly eased the process of buying for the innumerable buyers are over the world. They are sitting in their private residences and by only clicking a few buttons, can have absolutely anything delivered to them in a matter of hours. The facilitation is huge and a time may come when you also look forward to opening a store on the internet for your goods.

An important aspect to look out for before you can start on establishing an e-store, is to know exactly how are you going to bring customers in. In other words you to need to sell your online store before you can sell from it. According to the budget that you can spare, you can choose big marketing or free promotion in case the investment is supposed to be negligible.

Advertising is the basic step you can begin with. Fortunately for you, Google has provided its AdWords advertising to help you in this respect. Your site is advertised over the internet and the first line of customers start pouring in. Of course the advertising priority is based on the local competition and the level of professionalism and creativity that is shown by your content.

SEO promotion is a big step to achieve. You have to get your site recognized with the best standards of Search Engine Optimization protocols. This will ensure that according to the keyword searching for users around the world, your link is displayed at the top and you get an ever increasing traffic for your store.

Price aggregators are a long way to go. As a store owner, you must realize the competition you are in and so must prepare for a combating situation. For this purpose, you must get your prices in sites which tabulate and compare the prices for different items over the internet. These are the aggregators. Once there, you can get your share of customers if you offer better prices.

Socialization is as important as anything else. You can make use of the many social websites like Facebook, Twitter and others to promote your online store. This brings a lot of publicity and also opens new channels over which your store gets promoted.

Offline marketing is an essential part of the viral marketing for your online store. This might be bring out a local response of buyers, but it is worth having. You can make use of local billboards, newspapers, flyers and much more to increase awareness in your community about your online store. As before with social networking, this will result in paving new ways in front of you to spread publicity about your store.

Blogs and online forums are the next leap forward. You can utilize these spaces to generate buyers for your store.

There is great audience for content like these and so a whole new field of potential buyers opens up this way.

TV and radio are the perhaps the biggest steps of the ladder that you are climbing. This solely depends on the budget of your marketing scheme and the level of publicity that you have already achieved for your store.

21   Viral marketing for articles

Articles are a great way to speak up and let your personal message out their in the open in front of the whole wide world. It is a means to share your views and opinions, imagination or sometimes just facts with everyone who is on the world wide web. But getting an article to go viral on the internet is not as easy as it seems. To have your article pop up all over the search engine results when the keywords are typed is no simple task. It not only requires hard work, but also a mind set to be creative enough to do what is necessary in a formidable enthusiastic manner.

The first step is to **write the best** articles out there. You have to put up content that has never been read before and is simply brilliant. Make it interesting and fun so that your readers have a hard time getting their focus off of it after they start reading it. Choose or create an excellent title that compels the audience to get eager about reading what you have to say.

Make your article **memorable.** The easiest way to do this is to write a story. Stories have been in demand since the beginning of time and thus bring about a greater response for one. Choose your niche carefully and know your audience before you do.

Make sure your article is **correct.** There should be a tone of professionalism and no chance of error. The grammar and spelling mistakes should be double checked. The writing should be in perfect English or you will lose credibility.

Next step is to choose **good platforms.** Submit your articles to blogs and directories which are already having a great viral load. You can contact writers who are looking for guest writers in their teams and be a part of something great. There will be plenty of opportunities concerning bloggers related to your niche. You can post your articles on forums and social websites too.

Writing **multiple related articles** can create an extensive attraction for your marketing. You can group them together to create an e-book. You can even divide your big articles into smaller paragraphs and create an auto responder for readers which allow them to read your whole content in sequence. This creates an illusion of episodes and leave the people wanting for more.

It is also a good idea to make a **short video or animation** related to your articles. You can take the titles or theme keywords, add images and videos to create a powerful attractive tool at your disposal. It is bound to bring in more readers as now a whole new sector of audience has been contacted.

One of the best ways to expand your domain is to create an **mp3 version** of your articles. Most people do not have time to sit and read lines from books or interactive media like computers and smart phones. This way, they can listen to a narration of your worthy articles while jogging, working, traveling or doing anything in their day to day lives.

22 Viral marketing via Instagram

Social platforms are a great opportunity to do viral marketing through. They provide ample cover for attracting wider circles of audiences. The investment costs are negligible and the processes are easy to handle. It is simple to workup a plan through them to make your content recognized far and wide. Among the many social websites out there, Instagram is a social website that isn't given much credit. Although new in the competition, this site provides a new way of understanding and utilising marketing skills.

Advantages of using Instagram

- Instagram works based on picture posting. A picture is very valuable in making a solid point of something. Especially if the marketing is about stuff like food, weight loss, travel destinations or similar, pictures can say a lot more than words. People are generally more attracted to beautiful pictures as compared to lengthy and boring texts. A single picture can define what is to be explained in 2 pages full of words;

- The prospect of a picture going viral on Instagram is huge. This means more people not only viewing your

pictures but also sharing them with their friends and family. This expands the spreading message exponentially. The coverage is increased and the traffic to your content stacks up on itself;
- In the case of Instagram, the majority of work is handled by the followers of the picture. This is true as is evident nature of viral expansion through Instagram. This makes things easier for the you or your company as now you can focus your attention on something else while your followers make sure that new channels of marketing are opening for your each passing moment.

Disadvantages of using Instagram

- The audience of Instagram is for now mostly composed of young lot. This does not mean that your content and pictures will not gain the popularity they deserve. It just translates into your product gaining a stronghold in an audience with little to spend. So the overall marketing values from Instagram are a little less. The users of Instagram are not that business minded. They use it mostly in their idle time and its just to pass most of it. The actual percentage of those using Instagram for professional purpose is very low;
- Instagram is still pretty new in market and so it is difficult to get started quickly on finding the number of interested people that you ate hoping for. The starting of your project will be slow and a lot of patience is

needed to make only the initial numbers. This is opposed to the fact that other social websites like Facebook and Twitter are widely acclaimed in multiple territories and are easy to begin with.

Having discussed the pros and con's of using Instagram for viral marketing, it must be acknowledged that this social website is a must for the brightest of the entrepreneurs. The site is gaining popularity day by day and soon it will be on the front line for professional marketing techniques and gateways.

23 Hiring an agency for viral marketing

Viral marketing is the latest trend picking nowadays. It is the channel If choice for spreading your message far and wide over the internet. It has deep roots and extends to viral marketing of photos, videos, audio, articles, blogs and more. Viral marketing is all about getting people interested in what you have to offer and then spread the it

among family and friends over any platform possible. The rise in popularity is exponential and from a sales point of view, the profits are immensely increased over a negligible initial investment.

Most of the times, it is not that easy to initiate a project like this and then achieve the scores that you hope for in a specific time period that you have in mind. Fortunately for this, there are agencies you can hire that will do the viral marketing for you and help you in accomplishing wide acknowledgement of your product.

Why you should hire an agency

The obvious outcome is an explosion of incoming traffic to your website or product which means more sales in time. The audience will be interested which will lead to increased suggesting of the information about your product or website.

A major advantage of using an agency is having a permanent mark on people minds which creates a reputation of yours for a long time. It means that even for all your future endeavours, your company's name will be enough to start doing good once again.

Using a viral marketing agency helps you to achieve a worthy status among the big players in business world. As you get more and more people coming in, eyes will be set on your progress and new opportunities of expansion or merging open up.

Hiring an agency also helps you in multitasking. It helps you in focusing your attention elsewhere of your company and not worry about the marketing aspect at all. The more time you have at your end, the more creative you will be resulting into new, unique and fascinating creations. These will further help to achieve higher traffic incoming rates.

Why it could be difficult to hire an agency

There a cost of hiring a viral marketing agency. As is the case, the better the agency the higher its price. For those who are starting a business or a project for the first time, it is usually not possible to pay for an agency.

It is difficult to know for sure if the agency you are hiring is as good as it claims to be. The issue of complete trust comes into play. There is a chance of you spending your money on an agency that turns out to be fraud.

Thus it all depends on where you stand at working for your website or company. If you have a good enough balance at your disposal, you may hire a good company that can help you get to your goals faster. You may need to use good contacts that can help you to point out to trust worthy agencies and make your process easier and beneficial.

24 Utilizing free viral marketing Application

Viral marketing is being excessively employed to gain an increasing amount of traffic and promotion of companies, websites and products. It is being used to increase sales and make huge profits with as little an investment as possible. Fortunately for you there are great applications out there that you can run to make good reputation for you in the marketing regime. Most of these applications are paid. But discussed here is a great application for your viral marketing that is absolutely free.

Blastoff is a great app as the name speaks for itself. The application is still on beta phase it is new. This means that those of you who utilize it now will be pioneers and at the top of the wave that will rise to an unstoppable force in near future.

The application can be run on any browser. It is completely **customizable** and you can shape the interface to your exact liking. This is useful to make a comfortable environment to work in and put out your best potential forward. You can choose from among many widgets for the online stores. You can add tabs for watching television, movies, listen to music and play games. There is the option to change themes and colour schemes so that it is cool to the eyes to work on the browser.

The application works based on the **commission** system. It provides links of up to 300 travel sites and online stores from the most popular of brands including Dell, Apple, Walmart, Gap, Expedia and many more. For every purchase that is made through your site by any of these stores, you receive a bonus of the payment as your commission. You can start from 1 to 10 percent of the cash back on every single purchase. This means absolutely free money making from the efforts of others who use your site. Moreover at the end of the month, you also get a bonus check which means double the profits you already are making.

You can get an exponential increase in the profits by **sharing** the links to others. The more the people who use your site, the bigger the commission you receive every time a sale is done. You can utilize the social platforms at your disposal or use other methods to spread the message. The real beauty is in the fact that as your friends who are using your site, invite friends of theirs to use the site; you reap the rewards.

There is a level system through which the commission you receive increases. The deeper your **level**, the greater the rewards. This application is the future of shopping. Just like everything else, it has the potential to eliminate the brick and mortar of shops and convert them into an array of codes and ease of access.

25 Boost viral marketing of Blogs

Writing blogs is an excellent passion. You can write blogs online and share with the world in a matter of a few clicks. Boosting your blog traffic is now easier than ever with the latest facilities and services provided by a number of

websites and applications. Following are some of the ways in which you can score a high number of audience for your day to day blogs.

Always list your blogs in **blog directories.** This makes sure that your blogs are mentioned in the respective categories and it is easier for your audience to search for the blogs that you have written.

Make sure you reply to all of the **comments.** This provides a feedback to you and encourages your readers to open about their thoughts and opinions. This leads to a better understanding of what you have written and how you have written and provides a better talent in the future writings of yours.

Write **often.** People are always waiting for something unique and new and presenting to them exactly that, keeps them interested. They will have a focus set on your writings when done often and the followings of your blogs will be long term.

Use related **images.** People are more fascinated by the imagery that is attached to your blogs. This gives to them a vivid picture of what you are trying to say and thus makes your writings into more fun and excitement.

Provide **social** sharing options on all your posts. This is perhaps one of the most important job of yours. Providing these social buttons would make it easier for the readers to share your content with their friends and family leading to a higher traffic and audience.

You can go one step further and create an **application** for apple, windows and android phones. There should be gateways for people who use only one of the many media modalities be it a tablet. Giving your readers an ease of access will promote your content to far and wide and the channels of sharing increases.

You must remember to build important **relationships.** Get to know other bloggers and join the necessary social groups related to your work. You are sure to receive important tips, help and advice from those who are top ranking in these fields. It also helps to increase your popularity and further enhance the amount of traffic pouring in. It is a good idea to comment on other people's blogs so that they know your personal touching approach too. You can also post links of other people's blogs on your timeline and further increase your relationships with potential customers.

Translating your blogs to other languages is also a very good way to open up ways to newer circles and groups of audience. By doing this your content will not be limited to a region or language. A global audience is always bigger than a local one.

Search engine optimization is also a very important aspect of viral marketing. Make sure you use your keywords often. You should submit your blogs to each and every major search engine.

26   Viral marketing with Youtube

Advantages of using YouTube

Using YouTube is absolutely cost free. There is no price for uploading your videos and making them known and viral in the whole world. YouTube's audience is global. It is one of the few websites that is used in almost every part of the world simultaneously. If narrowed down to the category of video's websites, YouTube has the top figures of being watched.

YouTube has a viral effect. Every person who sees a video and enjoys it, makes sure to share it with his or her close friends or family. And so the spreading begins. YouTube provides all the necessary links automatically to the user so that the video is shared fast and easily.

YouTube video posting improves the Search Engine Result ranking. As more and more people watch your video, its link will be placed higher and higher in the search results for the related keywords. This leads to an exponential growth of the traffic to your video. YouTube also automatically makes a personalized channel for your uploaded video. This gives the option to the viewers to subscribe for your channel and with each new posting, they will be notified about the new added video.

Steps to make a good viral video

Making a video for YouTube is not that difficult. It all starts with creating a free account on YouTube and registering yourself in the community. You can start by formulating the goals for your video. You do not need to worry about the competitors against your videos out there. Its because with each of their videos being watched, the link to your video will be in the suggested video lists. You can use guides get good ideas about your video. Other than that, any unique idea that incorporates fun and excitement with understanding and intelligence is a great viral video.

When you post a video, make sure you give a detailed description about the content of that video. Every word used in that description is essentially a keyword which brings the chances of your video being searched, very high.

After that its pretty much the basics of any viral marketing. You need to make sure that you post often so that there is new and good available to your viewers soon. At the end of your video you can ask the viewers to comment, rate it like your video. Higher the number of people who comply to your request, higher the amount of traffic that you will get.

How to spread the message

You should post your YouTube video links to other platforms. There is no rule against it and you should make full use of it. You can share your videos on blogs, forums, social websites like Facebook and Twitter and many more. Make sure that you lessen the amount of advertisements that you put, and make the links more personal so that you do not run out of friends and family to like your videos.

27   Viral marketing of Music

Music is a great feature of most viral marketing schemes. It is the chosen way for most multinational companies and corporations. Even when not employed as a sole channel, it goes side by side to other marketing items like images, videos and more which promote the music as much as the marketing item itself.

Difference between music marketing and music promotion

Music marketing is not the same as its promotion. Music promotion is a behaviour modifying step. It forces your audience to not just like your music but also to start buying it for themselves. It is the logical forerunner of your music sales.

Music marketing on the other hand is the step before promotion. It is about getting the audience to like and love your music so much so that they want to hear it again and again to the point that they start buying it. But how do you get your listeners to like and trust your content?

The first step is getting your audience to know that you exist. For this you have to know where they are, what they are doing and what do they love. Then you can be present where they are exactly and get them to listen to what you have to offer. This not only includes their physical presence but also the social online platforms where they exist.

The next and perhaps the most important step is getting them to like your music. The biggest role played in this is of your personal touch. If you can show your listeners that you care about them, they will turn to trust you back. You have to provide them a motive behind your music. An inspiration for your music will get your audience to get more engaged behind your music. Make sure you respond to what they have to say about your music. Follow their comments and reply with a warm gesture. This leads to building up of trust which makes sure that your audience not only listens to your music but also get to the next step of buying your music which is characterized by music promotion.

Top online music marketing strategies

You need to have a good web design and its development. Your website is not a static platform but an interactive environment. People love to receive new updates and unique content postings often. Give them just that.

Social media marketing is as important as anything else. You need to draft a management plan where you can respond quickly to what your fans have to say about you. Music is an inspiration and you need to provide just that.

You can promote your music by making online video. This puts a vivid motion to your music. You can further enhance the traffic by blog promotion of your music.

Article writing may be a less popular way of viral marketing for your music but it is quite worthwhile. Articles for your music can reach far and wide and cover those groups of audiences that are limited to reading content modalities.

28   Viral marketing for amateurs

Viral marketing is an art that is essential for almost everyone nowadays. With the increasing traffic over the internet, almost every sale is now being conducted through the channel of online viral marketing. If you are thinking of stepping into this realm of marketing, following are some tips to guide you in the right direction.

The first step in this ever expanding business is almost always **free.** There is absolutely an absence of significant investment when you start the viral marketing of your content. The only resources that you will need to use are your thinking skills and creativities.

You must remember to use **unique** ideas in all your endeavours. This is not possible with you trying to mix up the current trends and trying to present something different with it. It is only feasible when you can create something out of your own imagination. This way, you can truly come into the competition of your rivals and have a shot at beating them.

Break down your content and **link** the individual pieces. Provide links to various sites and places in each one of your postings so that everything is inter connected. You can create parts and the links would take your audience to complete the second part of what you present. This is in accordance with the fact the people are depressed to watch the wordings, "to be continued" but are also impatiently waiting to watch the next episode.

Whatever you make should have the element of **fun** in it. It should be amusing and full of entertainment for people to enjoy. To heighten the emotions of your audience with each new concept paves the way to increased sharing and spreading of your content.

Offer free **bonuses** and tips to your audience. This opens up wider roads for your traffic to pour in. This is a must to have people keep their focus on what you have to present. This keeps them in the loop and promotes your content more than ever. You can also act as a freebie and provide free viral marketing. People love to get free information and this proves to be a plus for your viral marketing campaign.

Provide an appropriately huge resource **sharing** option. This keeps the viewers to link and share the content on their own websites and forums. But this also makes sure that all the shared content links back to your own website or content. This increases the channels that spread out your content and increase the incoming numbers of viewers.

Make short an beautifully crafted **videos.** You can post these videos on YouTube or any other social media sites. These videos provide a better way to promote your content and indulges in more people to participate in your the items that you have to offer.

You should know the important details of your designs and infrastructure so that you can avail the option of **outsourcing** it all later. If you fail to understand the critical patterns, you may get into trouble and have problems later.

29 Event promotion and destination marketing

Promoting an event has taken on new and better modalities since past couple of years. The use of old and traditional schemes like using online calendar entries in directories have generally been discarded. For most of the work today, there are available many event marketers, promoters and other similar niches that provide

a large impact of incoming traffic to your event promotion. There is also always the option to add in some flavor of utilising the social media for viral marketing of your event. There is a well-organized web of interconnected links between all the social platforms and marketers available by your side every step of the way.

Chases Calendar Of Events

This is one of the most fundamental and basic reference used by the traditional journalist and bloggers to cover all the necessary events in the future. This website provides the dates and schedule of all the major events including holidays, festivals, anniversaries, famous birthdays and many more. You can even post your own dates here absolutely free and get the required popularity.

Flickr

This is very good site that provides a vivid experience of past, current and future events. You can post pictures of any event you are looking forward too and expect to have a great response for it sooner than you can think. You can even post videos of the last year's events and give your audience something beautiful and creative to look forward to.

MeetUp

This site is all about what the name suggests. It provides you with the opportunity to invite whoever you like to events such as parties, marathon runs, art exhibitions, fun fares, wine tastings, social gatherings and much more. You can choose your audience to be as public or personal as you want. You can even arrange to have a space set up in your community to have meetings among the members of your MeetUps.

Craigslist

This site has earned a great name for itself in the viral marketing of events. It is very popular among a global audience with over 20 million page views per month. This site is divided among different categories including events, activities, classes, politicians, musicians and artists. There are also many hundreds of forums based on these sub categories. You can post your events according to one of the sub category or according to the city you are posting in.

Inflight Magazines

You can post your photos and event descriptions to the inflight magazines which share a large and diverse coverage of audience. The long flights make sure that what you have to present is read thoroughly and responded to more.

CitySearch

This is one the most popular sites for destination search. It has insider blogs and forums where you can share your recent visits and destinations. People have the option to search for nearly every place be it historic, sightseeing or business oriented. It also has details to insiders to which you can built relationships and be a step ahead of the competition.

30 Best Photos for viral marketing

Today can be rightly called an age of photography. Everybody is holding a camera or most likely a smartphone and is capturing every moment that is spent. If you want to post a photo that you want promoted virally, you just need to follow a few basic steps and your photo will be on its way to global popularity.

You can join **professional associations** that can help you to get where you want quickly. These groups can help you in almost every step including general guidance, photographic skills, editing techniques and much more. You can

look for local photographic clubs and societies that are better for a long term side by side placement.

It is essential that you join **social sites.** Nowadays the usage of the social websites is at the top level and this is perhaps the best way to get maximum attention. Instagram is the best site for posting good photos and getting high views but it is new as compared to the other sites and so you will get a less professional audience. Facebook and twitter are the pioneers of social networking and are sure to hand over a business minded audience that will get your photo the desired publicity.

It is important that you capture **good photos.** An important aspect in photography is the unique perspective of a photographer. Multiple photos taken by different people of the same object, will be different for each one of them. Some will be a close up, some will highlight the background, some will accent the focus with another object in the photo and so the diversity occurs. You need to find your own thing and you can improve on it. Good pictures can clearly indicate the focus of attention that is being sought.

Adding **humour** to your photos is a great way to increase the traffic for it. Everybody loves to laugh and people like those items that helps them celebrate life. Take for example an advertisement. Most people would choose to ignore it because they know that it has been posted solely for a selling purpose. On the other hand, they would surely open up a funny photo to view more like it.

Editing your photo is as important as taking one. There are many tools and software available both paid and free and for online and offline use. These provide ample options to create something magical out of every photo taken. One such software is VSCO Cam. It is in great demand nowadays and everybody is loving its use. It provides different flash modes for multiple environments. You can settle the focus and exposure to highlight the field of choice. There are many filters to pass your photo through and through them you can customize a great unique background for each of your photos.

Give a good **caption** to your photos. A good title or tagline gets the people to understand your photo better and thus incite interest. Most of the captions used nowadays are supposed to be a humorous contrast to the photo which produces some laughter leading to sharing of the photo.

www.ingramcontent.com/pod-product-compliance
Lightning Source LLC
Chambersburg PA
CBHW072231170526
45158CB00002BA/855